FOOD

AND COOKING IN PREHISTORIC BRITAIN

HISTORY AND RECIPES

Couch or Quitch

First published 1985
by the Historic Buildings and Monuments
Commission for England
© Jane Renfrew and HBMCE, 1985

Printed by CBE Design & Print, Birmingham
Designed by Elizabeth Mander

C100 10/85
ISBN 1 85074 079 8

FOOD

AND COOKING IN PREHISTORIC BRITAIN

HISTORY AND RECIPES
By Jane Renfrew

Illustrations by Peter Brears

English ✳ Heritage

Historic Buildings & Monuments Commission for England

Cleavers, Goose-grass   *Tansy*

Sweet Cicely   *Sorrel*

INTRODUCTION

any people might imagine that the task of re-constructing the diet of our prehistoric ancestors would be completely impossible. In some ways they are right, but when archaeologists recover the remains of our distant forebears and their tools they also look for clues about their foods. The process is essentially one of detective work and the direct evidence may survive in a variety of different forms: as mounds of discarded sea shells, the bones of wild and domestic animals (sometimes showing butchery marks, traces of burning during cooking, or split to obtain the marrow). The remains of plants are also often preserved mainly as seeds or fruits, having been charred in the past or buried in other conditions which favour preservation, as in waterlogged soils, or else having been preserved as impressions in clay vessels or in daub. So whether it be the hunters of the palaeolithic or the first farmers of the neolithic or the celtic chieftains of the late iron age, we do have quite a number of clues to help us reconstruct their diet. But having discovered the ingredients which were available, our task is to work out what could have been made from them.

A further lead in this quest is given by studying the tools used for food preparation–for cutting, grinding, pounding and for cooking. Thus we can begin to understand the range of cooking techniques which were available at any given time in our prehistoric past, and to see how they developed through time.

Another aid in reconstructing the methods used by pre-historic cooks is to examine the different practices which have survived in the more remote parts of the British Isles, where the inhabitants had to make do with much the same ingredients as were available in later prehistory. The ingenuity of the islanders of Orkney and Shetland, for example, serves to remind us that when the ingredients were limited in range it was up to the cook to make them varied, interesting and palatable: in the recipes which follow I have drawn on their experience too.

The first men appear to have arrived in Britain sometime before 300,000 years ago. These men were hunters and lived in the Pleistocene during which Britain was subjected to the advances of the polar ice-cap which reached at its maximum extent as far south as London; when, however, it periodically retreated the inter-glacial periods were extremely warm. Naturally these huge changes in climate and vegetation led to a great variation in the sorts of animals and plants which formed the food supply of the hunters and gatherers. In the cold phases the exposed parts of southern Britain appear to have been roamed by mammoth, woolly rhinoceros, reindeer, bison, musk ox and arctic hare. In the warmer interglacials these species were replaced by the straight-tusked elephant, the Clacton fallow deer, bear, wild oxen, red deer, rhinoceros, hyena and even in some places hippopotamus. Their bones have been found in association with the characteristic flint handaxe tools of these early stone age hunters. From the camp sites so far excavated there has been little evidence for the plant food part of their diet, but on analogy with modern hunting communities up to 80 per cent of their diet may have consisted of vegetable foods. These hunters led a nomadic life following the herds of animals which they relied on for meat. This pattern of shifting hunters and gatherers continued to occupy Britain throughout the palaeolithic. Their tool kit gradually improved and, by the upper palaeolithic, projectile points helped to make their hunting weapons more effective and they began to make sharp flint knives from long blades struck from the cores. At the end of the palaeolithic many of the inhabitants of Britain were living in caves and were hunting horses, reindeer, giant Irish deer, elk, arctic fox, woolly rhino and mammoth.

With the retreat of the ice sheets the climate became progressively milder, and after about 10,000 BC the tundra vegetation gave way to a forested environment, first of birch, hazel and pine and then of oak and other deciduous trees such as elm, lime and alder. With the spread of forest conditions the large herds of wild animals were replaced by forest species: red and roe deer, elk and wild oxen and wild boar. Those hunters who lived close to the sea also began to exploit shellfish and sea fish, leaving huge mounds of shells and fishbones as evidence of their taste for marine foods. Thus from about 300,000 to about 3,500 BC the inhabitants of Britain lived exclusively by hunting and gathering.

About 3,500 BC the first farmers reached Britain from the Continent by sea (the land bridge which had joined us to the Continent during the palaeolithic had become submerged after the melting of the ice sheets before 6,000 BC). These early farmers brought with them bags of seed corn comprising two types of hulled wheat (Emmer and Einkorn), and the hulled and naked forms of six-row barley, and flax. They also brought young domestic cattle, sheep, goats and pigs. Their completely new life-style included living in more or less permanent settlements, using pottery containers, weaving cloth, making polished stone tools and constructing elaborate tombs and ritual monuments. Their arrival brought a truly fundamental change in the way of life of the inhabitants of these islands, and they laid the foundations of society as we know it today. These first farmers set the stage for various technological developments, the most important of which was the development of metallurgy—first with the making of copper, then bronze tools and later with iron working too. These had implications for cooking since it was now possible to have a wider range of tools, especially sharper knives, and later buckets and cauldrons, flesh-hooks, firedogs, spits and tripods, spoons and elegant drinking vessels.

The recipes which follow are supposed to reflect the development of the prehistoric economy in Britain, but several practical restraints have had to be introduced. First, it is rather difficult to give recipes which might relate to the palaeolithic since it is clearly difficult to obtain the ingredients—mammoth steaks or rhinoceros joints for example. So I have confined the recipes to the early post-glacial period and from then on to the end of the iron age immediately preceding the Roman invasion. I have also included only those wild foods which can be fairly easily recognized and are relatively abundant, so that anyone following the recipes will not subject themselves to the misfortune of consuming unpalatable or even poisonous plants by mistake, or to collecting plants which though once common are now rare and should be conserved.

7

The main difference between prehistoric food and that of today is that our distant ancestors cooked rather simply; they did not go in for elaborate sauces and having few ovens did not bake pies. Also there are a number of ingredients which we habitually use today which were not available to them, among the most important of which are the following: yeast (except the wild forms), baking powder, cream of tartar, spices, lemons, oranges, grapes, wine, vinegar, olive oil, onions, tomatoes, potatoes and cornflour. They did not have sugar, but used honey for sweetening.

They did, however, use much more of our wild vegetation than we do now and their edible plants probably reflected seasonal availability much more than do our modern-day vegetables. One reason for this is that deep freezing and freeze drying preserve our vegetables out of season; in the past vegetables and fruits could only be preserved by air drying, or by being made into preserves such as jam or jelly, or alcoholic beverages such as mead. As far as we know most vegetable foodstuffs were not preserved on a large scale outside their season of availability. The one exception to this is grain, which was stored in pits to provide a steady food supply through the winter and up to the next harvest.

The same problem of preservation was also important for animal products. Meat and fish could be air dried, sun dried, salted or smoked to preserve them through the scarce winter months, and this has been practised until recent times in the islands off our northern coasts.

Another feature that strikes one when looking at the uses of animals, birds and fish in these remote places is that nothing was wasted: udder, lights, tripe, brains, head, feet, tails, blood and even gristle were made into dishes which may not sound appetizing to our rather refined notions today, but which would be quite acceptable in the absence of any alternatives.

Prehistoric Food Resources

The sea and seashore were important sources of food for those who lived near. The occasional stranding of whales round our coasts must have provided a great bonus to those living in the vicinity, and it is not uncommon for up to four whales on average to be stranded on British shores each year. Olaus Magnus writing in 1555 described how a single whale might fill between 250 and 300 waggons and yield meat for salting, blubber for lighting and heating, small bones for fuel and large ones for housebuilding, and hide sufficient to clothe forty men, so one can understand what a windfall such a stranding might be. Perhaps the earliest example of man's exploitation of this resource is from Meiklewood near Stirling in Scotland where a mesolithic deer antler mattock was found propped against the skull of a Rorqual whale. Seals were also exploited off the Scottish coast and their bones occur in the mesolithic middens in Argyll and on Oronsay.

The mesolithic inhabitants of Oronsay already practised deep sea fishing from boats: they caught and ate conger eel, sea bream, saithe, wrasse, haddock, thornback ray, skate and shark. At Morton, Fife, on the east coast of Scotland, the mesolithic fishermen were also catching cod, salmon and sturgeon. In the Orkney Islands during the neolithic they were catching cod and coalfish; and finds of crushed fish bones in a mortar at Skara Brae may suggest that fishmeal was used as a famine food. Fish was probably best eaten fresh, being gutted and grilled over an open fire, or baked in hot embers. A large fish would be cut into steaks to facilitate quick and even cooking. Fish roes and livers also constituted rich foods much valued in the northern isles.

Crabs and lobsters were collected along the edge of the shoreline, or just beyond it, probably in weighted baskets – the forerunners of modern lobster pots. They were certainly appreciated by the mesolithic inhabitants of Oronsay and Oban and have probably been valued ever since.

Around the shores of Britain are a series of sites which consist of huge middens of shells, the discarded remains of many meals of shellfish which have been widely valued by the communities living by or visiting the seashore. This is not quite universally true, since in Orkney they have traditionally regarded 'ebb meat' as a last resource in times of hardship. Gathering shellfish may well be regarded as rather labour intensive. The most common species represented are oysters, limpets, mussels, and winkles. It has been argued that the limpets may have been used as fishing bait, but since they are found in such large numbers some at least may have been used for food, possibly as a tasty addition to a fish stew or soup. Sea urchins were also used for food on the late neolithic/early bronze age site at Northton, Harris. All these shellfish are best cooked by dropping them into boiling water and boiling them briskly for a short while before extracting them from their shells. They may also be roasted on hot stones. As soon as the shells open a piece of butter is put inside each, and the shellfish eaten immediately.

Sea birds also formed an important source of food on the coastal sites. Guillemots were present in the mesolithic site at Morton, Fife. They were also present at Skara Brae in Orkney, and on the Rousay sites. Here also were found gannets, eider ducks and their eggs, pink-footed geese, and swans. There is no doubt that these birds were valued for food as well as for their feathers. The inhabitants of St Kilda in the eighteenth century caught guillemots and gannets and either ate them fresh or salted them for use during the long winter months. They also ate large quantities of the birds' eggs boiled.

No finds of seaweed are known from early sites but it is likely that laver, *Porphyra umbilicalis*, which grows in the intertidal zone on the rocky coasts of western Britain, and also carragheen or Irish moss, *Chondrus crispus*, were probably both used, as they are up to this day. Both species are rich in iodine and vitamins. Seakale, *Crambe maritima*, a plant growing on the shingle beaches round our shores yields delicate tender shoots which can be cooked and eaten like asparagus, and marsh samphire, *Salicornia europaea*, which grows on the sandy mud of salt marshes, has succulent fleshy

Seakale   *Marsh Samphire, Glasswort*

stems of delicate flavour when boiled. Both these plants may have been locally exploited but would leave no archaeological trace.

Inland, the hunters of the early post-glacial forests relied heavily on game animals for their meat supply. The mesolithic band which camped during the spring beside a lake at Star Carr, Yorkshire, were hunting red and roe deer, elk, wild ox and wild pig with the occasional wolf, pine marten, hedgehog and badger. The presence of domestic dog at this site suggests that it was used by the hunters in their food quest.

With the coming of agriculture, hunting still played a significant role in the seasonal food supply. Elk disappeared by the neolithic, and wild oxen by the end of that period. The neolithic farmers hunted wild ox, especially in southern Britain where their bones are often found associated with neolithic monuments. The commonest animal hunted, however, was the red deer, found on sites from the Orkneys to Dorset. Not only was it an important source of food, but it also supplied the huge numbers of antlers used as tools in the flint mines and in the construction of earthworks. In general, the red deer appear to have been much larger than contemporary Scottish deer. Of the other species of deer, both roe and fallow deer have been found on neolithic sites in the south and east of the country. Wild horse, wild boar, brown bear and beaver have all been found on neolithic sites also.

At Glastonbury during the iron age the farmers hunted red and roe deer, wild boar, fox, wild cat, otter and beaver, also hedgehog, marten, weasel and polecat. It was probably in the iron age that hunting was first regarded as a sport, with the celtic warriors decorating their shields with wild boar emblems to show their prowess in the hunt.

The meat of these game animals would have to have been eaten at once, or else hung for a long while to tenderize in which case it would have been eaten 'high' as it still is today. We must imagine that all parts of game animals were eaten in some form or other. The gut may well have been used as a container for liver, lights and brains cut up and mixed with fat, and then either slowly roasted over the embers of a fire, or boiled; it is a type of dish which survives as the Scottish haggis.

It is possible that the early hunters ate the half-digested contents of the stomachs of their quarry. They certainly broke open the mandibles and long bones of the animals they hunted to extract the marrow.

Of the wild birds hunted in the late upper palaeolithic, the bones found at Kent's Cavern, Torquay, show that grouse, ptarmigan, grey-lag goose and whooper swan were being hunted for food. The first farmers also hunted goose, swans and ducks. It is possible that the art of falconry began to be practised during the bronze age as an aid in catching birds for food. There are a number of burials in Yorkshire where an archer is buried together with a hawk's head, for example in the beaker grave at Kelleythorpe.

The long list of birds, predominantly aquatic species, which were hunted by the iron age fowlers of the Somerset Lake Villages include: pelicans (and their young), cormorants, herons, bitterns, puffin, whooper swan, goose, wild duck, golden eye, teal, widgeon, pintail, shoveler, tufted duck, scaup, common pochard, red breasted merganser and common crane. At Meare the bones of black and red grouse and partridge were also found. One should not overlook the importance of birds' eggs in the diet too, in the long centuries before the introduction of the domestic fowl sometime in the later iron age.

The mesolithic fishermen on the inland waterways caught

freshwater fish such as pike by using fish spears or leisters armed with barbed antler points. Fish hooks were not introduced till much later. Fish traps and the use of fish nets must have a long prehistory here, as they do on the Continent. At Glastonbury, lead net sinkers were quite common and the villagers caught roach, perch, shad and trout. Pike and salmon were still caught using fish spears since they are much larger fish.

The first domestic animals arrived in Britain around 3,500 BC with the first farmers. They must have brought young animals in their skin boats across the Channel. Herds of sheep and goats, cattle and pigs were soon established. It seems possible that there may have been some subsequent crossing between the long-horned domestic cattle and the wild ox of the native forest before that species died out at the end of the neolithic. A small breed of goat was identified in the animal bones from Windmill Hill, and the sheep appear to have resembled the long-tailed Drenthe breed of Dutch heath sheep. The pig is also of a small form which persisted in Britain at least until the iron age. Both cattle and pigs would be happy browsing in the clearings in the forest, the sheep and goats would thrive better on the well-drained uplands. There is no evidence for the domestication of the horse before the bronze age. The neolithic dogs were of the large fox-terrier type.

Cattle appear to have been the most significant of the neolithic domestic animals. At many of the causewayed camps in southern Britain large numbers of young animals (under the age of one year) appear to have been poleaxed – we may imagine that quite a lot of veal was thus available for eating. Many of their bones show knife cuts at points suitable for the removal of sinew, flesh and skin. Many of the bones were split for the extraction of the marrow. The high proportion of young animals killed also implies that there must have been a good supply of milk available for human consumption, either fresh or in the form of butter and cheese. In the winter months the cattle were probably bled, the blood being mixed with flour and herbs to make black puddings.

Pigs may have been given less attention in neolithic times and allowed to forage at will through the forests until needed to supplement the food supply. Not only did they supply pork but

Lady's Bedstraw   *Butterwort*

also lard which was used in many dishes. Pigs may have some-times been used, when confined in pens, to break up fallow land and manure it. If left long enough in a confined space they will even get rid of perennial weeds.

Sheep and goats were more important on higher ground, and they appear to have become more numerous during the later phases of British prehistory. Sheep were valued for mutton and for wool. Goats were probably kept for their milk as well as their meat.

Butter and cheese were milk products which could be kept for some time. Butter was probably made in much the same way as it was in the Orkneys until recent times. The milk was left to stand in the churn for two or three days until it thickened naturally. When the butter was slow in coming some red hot 'Kirnin' stones were thrown in to help the separation process. When the butter had gathered at the top it was lifted out into an earthenware dish and washed several times in cold water to remove any remaining milk, which would turn it sour quickly. It then had to be dehaired by passing a knife through it several times to remove any animal hairs on the knife edge. In many parts of Britain it was the custom to bury the butter in wooden vessels or baskets, or occasionally in cloth, bark or leather containers, in peat bogs. Many discoveries of

14

this 'bog butter' have been made, ranging in quantity from a few pounds to as much as a hundredweight. The most rational explanation for this is that the surplus summer butter was stored in the cool bog for use in the winter. One Irish writer records that unsalted butter flavoured with wild garlic used to be put in a boghole and left to ripen.

Cheese is made by heating thick cream and adding rennet, which was obtained from the stomachs of calves. Occasionally plants were used as a substitute for rennet: the leaves of butterwort, *Pinguicula vulgaris*, lady's bedstraw, *Galium verum*, and nettle juice have all been used for this purpose, the last two being used in making Double Gloucester cheese. Simple cottage cheese is made by standing the milk till it separates into curds and whey, straining the curds through a muslin overnight, and then emptying them into a bowl and adding chopped herbs and salt to flavour it. My Cumbrian great-grandmother used to bury it in the garden for a week or so to improve the flavour. It should then be eaten fairly quickly as it does not keep well.

Together with their domestic animals, the neolithic farmers brought bags of seed corn and introduced a range of crop plants. They were the first people to cultivate the land and reap their harvests in autumn, storing it in pits to serve as the food supply through until the next harvest. Their chief crop was the hulled wheat called Emmer, but they also grew a little Einkorn wheat and brought two forms of the hulled six-row barley. Thus wheat and barley which had first been domesticated in the Near East some thousands of years earlier were introduced to the British Isles, and they still form our major cereals (though we now cultivate different species of wheat with better baking qualities). Oats and rye were not introduced, as far as we know, before the iron age, but spelt wheat may have been introduced before the end of the bronze age. The free-threshing forms of breadwheat were also known from this time onwards. The coarsely ground husked grains could have been baked into small unleavened loaves on the hearthstone beside the fire, or they could have been made into porridge or gruel, or added to stews or soups, cooked in pots which the first farmers also introduced.

The weeds that grew in the cornfields were probably harvested with the grain and had a food value often comparable to that of the cereals. Moreover, they were often incorporated into the cereal-based pottage and added flavour to it. A richer, more interesting soup resulted from the addition of fat or oil to the pot. Animal fat, or the oil-bearing seeds of flax would have been used. When the stomach contents of the iron age Tollund and Grauballe man were examined in Denmark, it was found that they had eaten a last meal which consisted of a cereal-based pottage mixed with linseed and a large number of weed seeds from a wide range of species. When the stomach contents of our newly discovered Wilmslow man are analysed we should have direct evidence of some part of the diet of iron age man in this country.

Barley was also used for making malt, and brewing beer. It appears that this process may well have been discovered by the end of the neolithic, and that the appearance of elegant beakers indicate the popularity of this beverage. The process of making malt is well described for the Orkney islands. Bere grain (hulled six-row barley) was set aside for malt. It was put in a large tub and covered with water. It was left to steep for forty-eight hours, then the water was drained off. The damp grain was then spread out on the barn floor for two to three days until germination took place. The grain was then collected in a heap, and two or three people began rubbing off the shoots with their feet by shuffling slowly

Iron age tankard of bronze and wood from Trawsfynydd, Merioneth

round the heap, twisting their toes and heels alternately, working to the centre of the heap. The malt was again heaped up and covered with straw and a mat to induce heat and further fermentation–the grain showed renewed signs of life and emitted a strong liquorous smell. It was rubbed down again before being dried in the kiln. All that remained was the grinding of the malt on a quern. This was done in small quantities for immediate use–a stone or half a stone was enough for brewing–the rest was stored away in a dry place until required. The ground malt was put in a barrel and scalded with boiling water. After infusing for two hours the liquid was drawn off. For special occasions the ale was made more intoxicating by adding an oat sheaf to the must (some people preferred to add heather for this purpose). The liquor (wort) was boiled for about half an hour then it was strained again, cooled and set aside for some days to ferment with added yeast. When fermentation ceased the ale was drawn off and stored in barrels or bottles in a cool place.

The pulse crops, peas and small broad beans, first appeared in Britain in the bronze age, and although they were useful as a different type of seed crop, which could be stored for use out of season and provide both starch and protein, they were never to become as popular crops as the cereals. They had two main uses as foodstuffs. When dried they could be ground up and added to cereal flour for breadmaking in time of dearth and, chiefly, they

Neolithic pottery and spoons. Left to right: pottery vessel from beside Sweet Track, Somerset, found with alder or hazel spurtle or porridge stirrer; pottery spoon, late neolithic grooved ware bowl and an early neolithic pot

could be used in soups or stews, for when simmered in broth they burst open to absorb the broth and fat and become a palatable purée. Young peas could also be eaten fresh, as they are very sweet.

The surviving evidence does not shed much light on the plant species which were collected and cooked as green vegetables. From finds of seeds we may however conclude that fat hen, *Chenopodium album,* was widely used as a green vegetable, probably cooked like spinach. Nettles, too, are well represented and may well have been gathered as young leaves and made into soups or eaten boiled. Other plants which have palatable leaves and may be cooked in these ways include common orache, *Atriplex patula,* easter ledge, *Polygonum bistorta,* white dead nettle, *Lamium album,* cleavers, *Galium aparine,* charlock, *Sinapis arvensis* and wild cabbage, *Brassica oleracea.*

Edible roots may also have played a part as a source of food since early post-glacial times. They were probably used in winter. The following species have been eaten in the more recent past: dandelion, wild parsnip, wild carrot, yellow goatsbeard, sow thistle and silverweed. A note of caution should be added–the roots are often rather small and those from old plants may be bitter or tough. The tuberous roots of the pignut, *Conopodium denudatum,* and the truffle, *Tuber aestivum,* have been regarded as delicacies. The roots of couch grass, *Agropyron repens,* were used as famine food.

In the early part of the year a number of young plants yield edible leaves suitable for use in salads. These include hairy bitter-cress, yellow rocket, ivy-leaved toadflax, lambs lettuce, sorrel, wood sorrel, dandelion, red clover, wild basil, sow thistle, salad burnet (beware of its strong flavour) and wild marjoram. Remember that there was no oil or vinegar for the salad dressing.

Many wild plants have been used as herbs to add flavour to various dishes. We have definite evidence that the seeds of mustard, coriander and poppies were used as flavourings in pre-historic Britain. It is very likely that some of the following wild plants were also used. Onion flavour may be obtained from the new leaves and shoots of jack by the hedge, *Alliera petiola,* and from the leaves and bulbs of wild garlic or ransoms, *Allium ursinum.* A

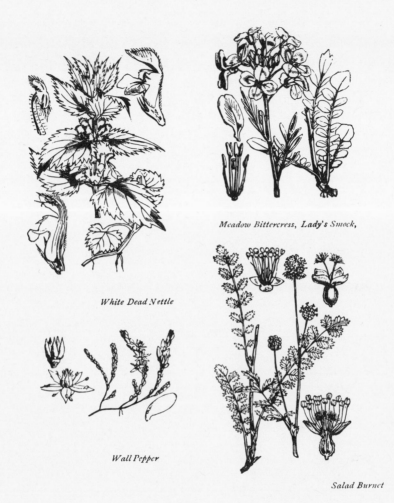

Meadow Bittercress, **Lady's Smock,**

White Dead Nettle

Wall Pepper

Salad Burnet

peppery flavour can be obtained from all parts of wall pepper, *Sedum acre,* and also from lady's smock, *Cardamine pratensis.* Sorrel leaves, *Rumex acetosa,* have a vinegary flavour. The leaves of salad burnet, *Poterium sanguisorba,* taste rather like cucumber, and those of sweet cecily, *Myrrhis oderata,* have an aniseed flavour. Corn mint, *Mentha arvensis,* tastes of mint, while water mint tastes of peppermint. The roots of herb bennet, *Geum urbanum,* have a strong clove flavour, and all parts of tansy, *Chrysanthemum vulgare,* have a strong flavour of ginger. Juniper berries form a good savoury spice.

Lime-tree

Pleasant drinks or tisanes can be made by pouring boiling water over the dried flowers of lime, elder, chamomile or woodruff, the fresh flowers of gorse, and mint leaves.

We have few remains of mushrooms or fungi from our prehistoric past, but an interesting exception is the find of a number of mature puffballs in the midden of the neolithic village of Skara Brae. These may have been discarded because they were overripe to use as food. Mushrooms are a useful source of food since they contain more protein than vegetables and a significant amount of vitamin D. They can easily be dried and stored for use out of season.

Before picking mushrooms to eat it is essential to become familiar with their identifications: there are about 3,000 species of fungi growing in the British Isles and only twenty of them are poisonous, of which four are fatally so. The following species are edible and fairly easy to identify (please refer to a good manual if you are not absolutely sure), they can be made into soups, added to stews or served in omelettes: morels, chanterelles, shaggy ink caps, saffron milk caps, shaggy parasols, ceps, blewits, field mushrooms, puffballs, beefsteak and oyster fungus.

All the fruits and nuts found on prehistoric sites in Britain belong to wild species. Many mesolithic camp sites have yielded large numbers of hazelnuts, suggesting that they were collected for winter use. The native woodland was rich in fruit- and nut-bearing trees whose produce was eaten fresh in due season: acorns, beechmast, hazelnuts, sloes, rosehips, haws, rowan berries, crab apples, wild pears, elderberries, strawberries, raspberries, blackberries and cranberries have all been found on prehistoric sites in Europe. In England, a beaker burial in the clay of the submerged coastline off Walton-on-the-Naze, Essex, was found to have about a pint of fruit seeds in the stomach region: these were chiefly the seeds of blackberries, mixed with rosehips and the seeds of *Atriplex*. We know from the impressions of apple pips in their pottery, that the first farmers ate crab apples. At Glastonbury the villagers had clearly been eating sloes – one mound produced nearly a barrow load of sloe stones. All these fruits can be used to make a storable jelly. In most cases it is necessary to add an equal amount of crab apple to the fruit in order to get enough pectin to make the jelly set. It is made by first bringing the fruit to the boil and simmering until mushy, it is then strained through muslin to separate the juice from the fibres and seeds. Measure the volume of liquid obtained and add to it an equal amount of honey. Bring to the boil, stirring well, and boil rapidly until the setting point is reached (220°F/104°C on a jam thermometer). Pour into sterilized jars and cover with waxed paper. When cool cover tightly with cellophane and store in a cool place.

Crab apples may have been made into verjuice and cider in prehistoric times. Verjuice would have formed a useful substitute for vinegar which was not known before the advent of the Romans. It is made by gathering the crab apples in a heap to sweat, discarding the stalks and any showing signs of decay. The apples are then mashed, using if possible a cider press to extract the juice. The liquid is then strained and stored for a month before it is ready for use. Crab apples were probably also halved and dried for use in the winter.

Crab Apple

Exotic early bronze age drinking cups. Left, amber cup found at Hove; right, the Rillaton gold cup

Honey was the only form of sweetening used in prehistoric Britain. We know from rock paintings that wild bees' nests were raided for honey in the late palaeolithic, and it seems likely that bees were actually being kept at least by the middle bronze age, for great quantities of wax were required for the casting of complex tools and weapons by the lost wax method. Wax would also be useful to seal up jars of jelly, verjuice, ale and mead for storage. Honey and salt were traditionally used together to season roast meat and fish in Ireland.

Mead was almost certainly produced in prehistoric times. Honey if left for a time will ferment of itself, and honey and water left together in a container would have produced an alcoholic drink, which could be flavoured with wild fruits and herbs. Traces of mead flavoured with cranberries and bog myrtle have been found in a birch bark container in a bronze age burial in Denmark. At Methilhill, near Kirkcaldy in Scotland, Mrs Camilla Dixon identified the pollen of small-leaved lime and meadowsweet inside a beaker in a grave. It appears that the beaker originally held mead made from lime honey and flavoured with meadowsweet flowers. Interestingly, the small-leaved lime does not grow nearer than the English Lake District, and so either honey or mead had been transported quite a distance.

Pots with perforated bases have been noted at several iron age sites and it has been suggested that they were honey strainers for separating the comb wax from the honey; examples come from Glastonbury and All Cannings Cross.

Cooking Techniques and Utensils

The use of preheated stones for cooking goes back at least to the mesolithic; Dr Paul Mellars has found deposits of fire-cracked pebbles in small pits in the mesolithic site in Oronsay. In the bronze age and later there is a whole category of sites known as 'mounds of burnt stones' which have been found from the New Forest to the Orkneys, in Wales and southern Ireland too. They appear to have been cooking places concerned with either (and more usually) boiling or roasting meat. Quite often they are found associated with a large watertight trough in which the meat was boiled. The technique of boiling/stewing in this way has been demonstrated by the late Professor O'Kelly in Ireland. A leg of mutton was wrapped in straw, tied securely with straw ropes, and lowered into boiling water in the trough. The water had been brought to the boil by successively dropping in red-hot stones which had been heated in a log fire beside the trough. The stones were transferred, with the ash, into the trough using a dampened wooden shovel, and in this way the water in the trough

Interior of neolithic house at Skara Brae.
A: hearth, B: bakestone, C: water-tight stone boxes,
D: saddle quern, E: stone dresser, F: knocking stone

was brought to the boil in about half an hour. Another stone was put in every few minutes to keep the temperature up. The 10 lb leg of mutton took 3 hours 40 minutes to cook in this way, and the trough which at first appeared enormous for its task was almost completely full of stones and ash. When the joint was removed it was found to be cooked through to the bone and was uncontaminated by the ash from the pot boilers.

As an addition to this experiment, Professor O'Kelly tried a different technique: that of roasting in a stone-lined pit. It was preheated by burning brushwood inside it, and then, after the ash was drawn out, another 10 lb leg of mutton was placed inside and surrounded by a rough dome of red-hot stones, preheated in a fire. Within twenty minutes the joint was sealed with a crisp brown crust which retained all the juices. The covering stones were changed seven times during the 3 hours 40 minutes cooking time, and at the end of the cooking time the meat was pronounced 'excellently cooked and most tasty'. The labour-intensive nature of the cooking must have given all concerned a good appetite.

The boiling of beef in a hide using pot boilers continued in some remote Scottish islands until the eighteenth century. Another method was outlined by Captain Edward Burt, who described how they put water into a block of wood which had been hollowed out with the help of a dirk and by burning. Then, using fairly large stones heated red-hot and successively quenched in the vessel, they kept the water boiling till the food was completely cooked.

In the prehistoric huts on Dartmoor each hut has a hearth sunk into the floor, and these are generally associated with heaps of

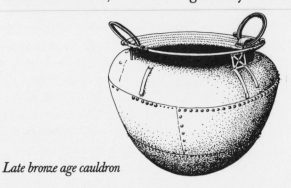

Late bronze age cauldron

*Late bronze age flesh-hook from Dunaverney, Co Antrim,
probably used for removing food from cauldrons*

fire-cracked pebbles, showing that pebbles heated in the hearth
played an important part in cooking and in boiling water even
round the domestic hearth. At Legis Tor a round-based pot was
still in position in one of the stone-lined cooking holes, and had
inside it a fire-cracked flint.

The most usual way of cooking meat was by grilling or
roasting it over the red-hot embers of the fire, using some sort of
spit. This need not have been more elaborate than a straight green
pole or stick, barbecue fashion, resulting in the meat having an
appetizing charcoal flavour when ready to eat. By the iron age,
elegant firedogs had been developed which may have also
supported spits.

The need for large containers for making stews was met
in the late bronze age by the introduction of huge bronze cauldrons
and their related hooks, chains and tripods for suspension over the
fire. The meat was fished out from these vessels with elaborate,
long-handled flesh-hooks.

One of the most extraordinary features of the prehistoric
houses which have been explored is their lack of ovens. It is not that
our prehistoric ancestors did not know about ovens, since we
know of a number of examples from the neolithic in Orkney at the
sites of Rinyo and the Links of Notland where there were small
ovens beside the central hearth, but they were not found
universally necessary. Even in the iron age villages of Glastonbury
and Meare where every house was furnished with a central hearth,
there are only two or three ovens in the whole village, and these
were probably associated with some occupation other than
cooking food. The exception is at Maiden Castle where three
ovens were found in a single house. Thus, baking in ovens was not
a commonly practised technique in prehistoric Britain.

Saddle quern
for grinding grain

Baking appears to have been done on a flat stone or bake-stone placed on or beside the central hearth. Sometimes bread may have been placed under an inverted pot which had hot embers piled over it. Emmer and Einkorn wheat do not make flour which stretches very much in the dough, and are thus better for making flat bread rather than leavened bread, though wild yeast may have been used to lighten the bread a little and add flavour to it.

The preparation of cereals for eating involved the use of pestles, mortars and querns. The houses at Skara Brae clearly show these two implements. The neolithic querns were of the saddle type with a bun-shaped upper stone which was rubbed backwards and forwards over a flat stone base. Rotary querns were introduced only in the iron age. They consisted of two circular stones: the lower with a convex upper surface and the upper with a concave lower surface, and a central hole through which the grain was fed. To prevent the upper stone slipping off the nether stone during grinding, a pin was fixed in the top of the nether stone and passed through a narrow bar of wood which crossed the feeding hole. At one side of the top stone a hole was drilled for the insertion of a wooden handle. The proximity of the two grindstones could be controlled by the insertion of leather washers under the wooden crossbar. In more recent times in Orkney the washer was inserted when oatmeal or malt was being ground, but not for the grinding of the finer barley meal.

Grain could have been prepared in three ways. It could have been prepared like graddan in the Hebrides up to the eighteenth century: a handful of ears of corn was held over the flames by the stalks, and the grains were beaten off at the moment when the husk was burnt but before the grain became charred. It was then winnowed and ground and baked within an hour of being harvested. Oats were 'burned in the sheaf' in a similar manner in Ireland in the past.

Another method was to make toasted grain, or 'burstin' as it is called in the Orkney islands. Barley grains were put in a pot beside the fire and the pot was tilted over on one side. To get the grains evenly dried and browned it was constantly stirred, and any which became burnt were discarded as they would give the burstin a dark colour and bitter taste. After being thoroughly toasted the grain was well sieved and then ground.

For making porridge or thickening soup the Orcadians used to use handfuls of threshed barley grains which were put in the 'knocking stane' or mortar with a little warm water, and were then lightly bruised with a mallet to break the husk. The husks were floated off by steeping in water and the grains were used just like pearl barley today. Last century boiled cabbage and 'knocked corn' formed a substantial part of the diet of these islanders.

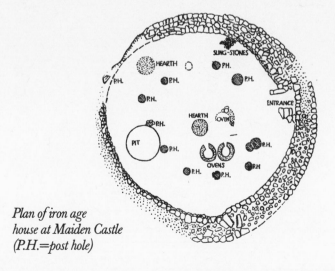

*Plan of iron age
house at Maiden Castle
(P.H.=post hole)*

Serving Prehistoric Food

Apart from flint-bladed knives there is little evidence of the eating equipment of our mesolithic ancestors, though they may well have had containers made from leather or wood from which they ate their meals. The first farmers introduced the use of pottery for storing, cooking and eating their food. The earliest pottery forms were round-based undecorated bowls – gradually through time impressed decoration began to appear round the necks and shoulders of the bowls. The round bases would have been more practical on an uneven floor, and in houses with no tables. By the late neolithic two types of flat-based pots, decorated with grooves or impressions over most of their surfaces, had become fashionable: the so-called Peterborough and grooved ware. The finds of pottery ladles from Sussex suggest that spoons may also have been made of wood, bone or horn, and a wooden spurtle was found in a bowl associated with the Sweet Track in the Somerset levels. A horn spoon was found in a beaker at Broomhead, Aberdeen.

The very finest prehistoric pottery made in Britain appeared in the late neolithic in the form of beakers, which seem to have been drinking vessels and are usually found in graves. They are

A beaker and two beaker mugs

An early bronze age vessel which may have been used as a salt pot

made from fine-grained clay and were decorated with horizontal bands of impressions made with finely toothed combs. Some of these beakers have handles and look as if they are copies in clay of wooden tankards. We know that the beaker from Methilhill, Scotland, had contained mead. It is possible that they may have also been used for ale.

Drinking cups made from exotic materials are a feature of the early bronze age in Britain: the Rillaton cup was made of gold, the Hove cup was carved from a single piece of amber, and two cups carved from shale were found near Amesbury, Wiltshire. One has to ask whether these materials were used in order to reflect the importance of the people using them, or of the liquid to be drunk from them.

The pottery of the early bronze age falls into two groups: the highly decorated flat-based, carinated bowls known as food vessels, and the larger urns with decorated rims and collars usually described as cinerary urns. Both are found associated with burials and so we cannot be sure that they have anything to do with food. Frequently associated with the large urns are small 'incense' or pygmy vessels. They often have holes for suspension and are decorated all over. Some are perforated, others have lids. I wonder if they could have been used for salt, since we now have evidence for the exploitation of salt in East Anglia at least as far back as the early bronze age. It would have been extremely valuable as a condiment to add piquancy to the bland food usually cooked.

The late bronze age saw the introduction of beaten metal vessels – notably, from the culinary point of view, the cauldron and the bucket. At this time also bronze knives were made, although flint continued to be used to make cutting tools into the iron age.

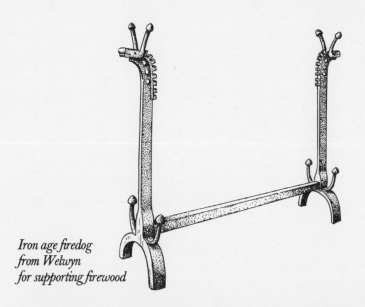

Iron age firedog
from Welwyn
for supporting firewood

Some of the early iron age pottery was decorated with a bright red haematite slip to make it resemble the burnished bronze vessels which were still luxury items. Some of the decorated pottery of the middle and late iron age is also rather attractive, especially that manufactured by the villagers of the Somerset levels, which is decorated with flowing lines and curvilinear patterns. The same style of decoration is also found on the wooden tub from Glastonbury. Here too were found both flint- and iron-bladed knives, and ladles and spoons made of wood. The curvilinear decoration is also to be found on the handles of bronze spoons which are characteristically found in pairs in Ireland and

Iron age bowl from
Glastonbury Lake
Village made
from bronze

northern England, and also on the handles of tankards, for example from Trawsfynydd, Merioneth. The cast-iron firedogs such as those from Capel Garmon, Denbigh, Welwyn, Hertfordshire, and Lord's Bridge, Cambridgeshire, were also works of art with their animal head terminals, and serve to underline the importance of the hearth to the iron age chieftains. Cauldrons, their hooks, chains and tripods, also feature at this time and are often found in graves.

In the first century BC the potter's wheel was introduced, and the pottery became much more stereotyped. Pedestalled bowls, platters, handled tankards and jars with countersunk handles became common pottery forms.

The rich burials of the Belgic chieftains show that already they had contact with the Roman world and were beginning to appreciate imported wine and olive oil. The grave goods found with the two burials uncovered at Welwyn at the beginning of this century include Mediterranean amphorae which must have contained wine, together with bronze and silver vessels for serving and drinking wine, firedogs, spits, and tripod cauldron hangers, pottery and wooden vessels – emphasizing the importance of feasting and drinking.

Future excavations, especially of waterlogged habitation sites, will no doubt shed new light on the foods, techniques of preparation, methods of cooking and serving of our prehistoric ancestors, but we have enough evidence to give us a glimpse into the way they utilized their available resources to provide an interesting and varied diet.

Wooden tub (left) and ladle from Glastonbury Lake Village together with a pottery bowl from Meare. Iron age

*A pottery urn (centre) and two pottery
food vessels from the early bronze age*

RECIPES

The recipes which follow are based on recipes drawn from the following sources: pease pudding from Elizabeth Ayrton, *The Cookery of England*; roast goose, fried pike, grilled salmon, grilled ox tails, marrow bones, grilled breast of mutton from *Mrs Beeton's Cookery and Household Management;* leaven, Yorkshire riddle bread, flowerpot bread from Elizabeth David, *English Bread and Yeast Cookery*; roast venison from Jane Grigson, *English Food*; frumenty, nettle purée, tansy pudding from J. Hill, *The Wild Foods of Britain*; laverbread, carragheen sweet mousse, boiled samphire, easter ledge pudding from R. Phillips, *Wild Food*; slott, crab, blaanda bread from J. Simmons, *A Shetland Cook Book*; fish soup, hakka muggies, sowans, porridge, burstin and milk from M. B. Stout, *The Shetland Cookery Book*.

FISH SOUP

trimmings and head of a large fish
1 small haddock
salt
seasoning (optional)
flour
milk

Thoroughly clean the trimmings and put in a pan with the haddock. Cover with cold salted water. Bring slowly to the boil and skim. Add seasoning (if using), simmer for 40 minutes, strain and return to the pan. For every 2 pints (1.1 litres) stock, mix 2 tbls (30 ml) flour to a paste with some milk and add to the soup to thicken it. Bring to the boil, check seasoning and serve.

HAKKA MUGGIES

1 fish stomach (a ling muggie is best)
1 cod liver
seasoning
oatmeal

Wash the muggie carefully, and tie the small end tightly with string. Break up or slice the cod liver, season well, and fill the muggie with alternate layers of liver and oatmeal until two-thirds full. Close, leaving enough room for the oatmeal to swell, and tie tightly with string. Plunge into boiling salted water and boil gently for 25-30 minutes. Remove from the water, and serve hot with bread.

GRILLED HADDOCK

Have ready a clear red fire; allow one medium haddock per person. Gut the fish and then lay them on a grill across the hot embers. Allow to grill first on one side, then turn over and grill the other side. Rub with a pat of butter and serve immediately. The haddock may also be toasted in front of the fire, retaining all the juices and the flavour of the fish.

SLOTT

1 cod roe
flour
salt

Beat the roe until creamy, then add a little flour and salt and form into small dumplings. Drop them into boiling well-salted water, and cook for 20-25 minutes. When ready they will rise to the top. Eat hot, or when cold cut into slices and fry in butter.

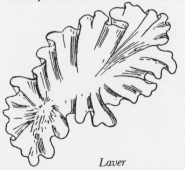

Laver

LAVERBREAD

Collect a good basketful of laver, avoiding any that are sandy. Break up the large pieces and wash thoroughly in cold water. Cook steadily for about 4 hours in a large pan of boiling water, checking every 30 minutes that it does not boil dry. It is cooked when the sheets of laver have broken up into tiny pieces, forming a smooth purée. Drain away excess liquid and store the puréed laverbread in the fridge until required. It will keep fresh for about a week. It is best served warm on fried bread garnished with bacon, since this helps complement the unusual texture and appearance of this excellent food.

SEA URCHINS

Sea urchins are usually eaten boiled like an egg. Boil briskly in salted water for 5 minutes. Drain, then open the urchins by cutting the concave side. Drain completely, discarding the excremental parts. To eat, dip buttered bread fingers into the yellow substance clinging to the inside of the shell. Sea urchins can also be eaten raw, as they are nowadays in the region around Marseilles.

CRAB

Choose a crab that is heavy in proportion to its size. Wash well and remove any adhering seaweed. Fill any holes in the shell with bread to prevent the meat becoming waterlogged in cooking. Drop into boiling salted water and cook for 15 minutes. When cold, break off the claws and take out the body – discard the green parts, gills and stomach. Chop the white and brown meats and arrange separately within the crab shell. Serve with warm bread rolls or bannocks.

BOILED SAMPHIRE

Samphire is a great delicacy. Pick marsh samphire during July or August at low tide. It should be carefully washed soon after collection and is best eaten very fresh. Tie the washed samphire, with the roots still intact, in bundles and boil in shallow unsalted water for 8-10 minutes. Cut the string and serve with melted butter. Eat the samphire by picking each stem up by the root and biting lightly, pulling the fleshy part away from the woody core.

CARRAGHEEN SWEET MOUSSE

¼ oz (7g) dried carragheen
1 pt (575 ml) milk
1 egg, separated
½ oz (15g) sugar or honey
fresh raspberries, to decorate (optional)

Soak the dried carragheen for 15 minutes in water, then pick out the dried ends and discard the water. Add the carragheen to the milk in a saucepan and slowly bring to the boil. Simmer for about 10 minutes, or until the mixture is quite thick. Beat the egg yolk with the honey or sugar. Strain the carragheen mixture and add the honey mixture to it. Beat the egg white until stiff, then fold into the mixture, stirring well, and pour into a bowl to set. The mousse takes 2-3 hours to set. It is nice to eat by itself, but is excellent with fresh or stewed fruit. If you omit the egg the mixture will set just as well and make a nourishing blancmange.

Carragheen (Irish Moss)

FRIED PIKE

1 pike, weighing 3-4 lb (1.4-1.8 kg)
salt
flour
1 egg, beaten
dry breadcrumbs for coating

Scale and clean the pike
thoroughly, removing the head
and tail. Cut the fish into slices
and cover with very cold water.
Remove when the fish feels firm.
Dry well and rub lightly with salt
and flour. Brush the slices of pike
with the beaten egg, then coat in
breadcrumbs. Fry in shallow fat
for about 30 minutes until tender.

GRILLED SALMON

2-3 slices of middle cut salmon
2 tbls (30 ml) melted butter
salt
parsley butter, to garnish

Wipe the fish with a damp cloth,
then brush with melted butter.
Season with salt to taste. Place the
fish slices on a well-greased grill
rack, and grill for 6-8 minutes on
each side according to thickness.
Serve immediately, garnished
with parsley butter.

ROAST VENISON

Venison is inclined to be hard and
dry unless carefully cooked. Lard
the joint and tie a jacket of fat
pork round it to retain the
moisture. It may be roasted on a
spit, but it is probably more
convenient to roast it in the oven
at gas mark 4, 350°F (180°C),
allowing 30 minutes per 1 lb
(450g). Serve with wild
mushrooms and rowan jelly.

MARROW BONES

8 oz (225 g) marrow bones per serving
flour
salt
dry toast, to serve

Scrape and wash the bones and
saw in half across the shaft (the
butcher will do this for you).
Make a stiff paste of flour and
water and roll it out. Cover the
ends of the bones with the paste,
to seal in the marrow, and tie the
bones in a floured cloth. Stand
upright in a pan of boiling salted
water and simmer slowly for
about 2 hours, refilling the pan
with boiling water if necessary.
Untie the cloth and remove the
paste from each bone. Fasten a
paper napkin round each one and
serve with dry toast.

ROAST GOOSE

2 oz (50g) butter
salt
1 young goose (up to 4 months old)
watercress, to garnish

Mix the butter and salt together
and place inside the bird. Truss,
and cook in a moderate oven, gas
mark 4-5, 350-375°F (180-190°C)
for about 1 hour, basting if
necessary. Place the bird on a
serving dish and garnish with
watercress. Instead of roasting in
an oven the goose could be spit
roasted over an open fire.

GRILLED OX TAILS

2 ox tails
1½ pt (850 ml) well-flavoured stock
1 egg, beaten
dry breadcrumbs for coating
melted butter

Wash and dry the ox tails and
divide them into pieces at the
joints. Put into a saucepan with
the stock. Simmer gently for
2½ hours until tender. Drain well
and leave until cold. Dip the ox
tail pieces into the egg, then coat
with the beadcrumbs. Brush with
melted butter and grill until
browned.

GRILLED BREAST OF MUTTON

1 breast of mutton
salt

Divide the breast into serving
portions. Remove surplus fat and
skin and season the mutton with
salt. Grill quickly under a hot grill
or over hot embers to seal the
surface, then reduce the heat and
grill for a further 15-20 minutes,
turning the meat frequently.

CUTLETS OF WILD BOAR

Sauté the cutlets in oil or butter
until tender, and arrange them on
croutons of fried bread. Pour
over them the pan juices mixed
with a little thick cream and a few
crushed juniper berries (1-2 per
cutlet). Serve with unsweetened
apple sauce.

Juniper

PEASE PUDDING

Originally the peas were probably tied in a floured cloth and hung to cook in the cauldron in which a large piece of pork was being boiled.

8 oz (250 g) dried green peas, soaked overnight
a few sprigs of mint and thyme
1 oz (25 g) butter
salt

Boil the peas in water with the herbs until soft and the skins are well loosened. Drain thoroughly and put through a sieve or blender with the butter. Add salt to taste. Press into a well-greased pudding basin, cover tightly with foil and steam for 1 hour. Turn out carefully, and serve with meat.

NETTLE PURÉE

Put young nettle tops into boiling water and boil until tender. Drain well and chop finely. Reheat, adding butter and salt to taste. Sorrel, dandelion, spinach, sow thistle, watercress and lady's smock may all be mixed for this purée (if the more bitter herbs dandelion and sow thistle are used alone, change the water after 5 minutes boiling). Cooking in a liberal amount of fast-boiling water will conserve the vitamins better than slow, gentle cooking.

SOWANS OR VIRPA

1 lb (450 g) fine oatmeal
3 lb (1.4 kg) wheatmeal
16 pt (9 L) water

Put both meals in a stone crock. Stir in 14 pints (8 litres) lukewarm water and let it stand for 5-8 days until sour. Pour off the clear liquid and let this stand a few more days until rather sharp: this is the swats, which makes a refreshing drink. The remainder in the crock will resemble thick starch. Add about 2 pints (1 litre) water to give the consistency of cream. Strain through a cheesecloth over a colander. The liquid which is passed through will contain all the nutritious properties of oatmeal, with only the husk remaining. Gentle rubbing with a wooden spoon and a final squeezing of the cloth by hand will hasten the process. This dish is good for invalids.

FRUMENTY

Half fill a jar with wheat grains, wash them, then cover with milk or water and set in a warm oven for 12 hours. The grains will swell and burst, and in this state are known as creed wheat. Frumenty may be eaten with cream and honey.

EASTER LEDGE PUDDING

1 lb (450 g) young bistort leaves and
nettle tops (dandelion leaves and
lady's mantle may also be used for
added flavour)
4 oz (125 g) pot barley, washed
salt
1 egg
a large knob of butter

Chop the greens and sprinkle the washed barley among them, adding some salt. Boil in a muslin bag for about 2 hours. Before serving, beat the mixture in a bowl with the egg, butter and salt to taste. Form into cakes and fry in shallow fat. Recommended as a good spring tonic.

PORRIDGE

1 pt (575 ml) water
a pinch of salt
2 oz (50 g) oatmeal
milk and honey (optional), to serve

Bring the water to the boil and add the salt. Sprinkle in the oatmeal very gradually, stirring well after each addition, then bring to the boil. Boil gently for 20 minutes if using fine oatmeal or 30 minutes for coarse. Serve with cold milk, and honey if desired.

BURSTIN AND MILK

Burstin is made from hulled six-row barley grains which are dried in a pot by the fire until roasted and then hand ground on a quern, making a rich brown meal. Put the burstin meal in a basin, heat some milk and pour over. Serve hot. This may also be made with cold milk or with buttermilk.

TANSY PUDDING

½ pt (275 ml) milk
½ oz (15 g) butter
3 oz (75 g) fresh white breadcrumbs
1 oz (25 g) sugar or honey
2 tsps (10 ml) finely chopped tansy
leaves
2 eggs, beaten
honey and cream, to serve

Boil the milk and butter together and pour over the breadcrumbs. Set aside for 30 minutes. Add the sugar or honey and the tansy leaves to the eggs, then mix with the breadcrumbs and bake the mixture in a moderate oven, gas mark 4, 350°F (180°C), until set. Eat cold with honey and cream.

BLAANDA BREAD

10 tbls (150 ml) barley meal
10 tbls (150 ml) oatmeal
a pinch of salt
2 oz (50 g) butter
milk, to mix

Mix the two meals and the salt in
a bowl, then rub in the fat.
Gradually add the milk to make a
dough which is firm but not
sticky. Shape into a round flat
bannock and bake slowly on a
griddle over the fire.

FLOWERPOT BREAD

1 lb 6 oz (600 g) wheatmeal flour
½ oz (15 g) leaven (see below)
½ oz (15 g) salt
about 12-15 fl oz (350-425 ml) milk
    and water, mixed

For these quantities use two
terracotta flowerpots, about
5½ inches (14 cm) in diameter.
Temper the pots by coating with
oil and putting into a hot oven.
Repeat this process three or four
times. Once the pots are well
sealed they will need very little
greasing.
Mix the ingredients together to
make a dough. Leave to rise for
2 hours, work the dough, then
leave to rise again for a further
2 hours. Divide the risen dough
between the pots and leave to

prove for 45 minutes. Invert on a
baking sheet and bake for 30
minutes at gas mark 7–8, 425–
450°F (220–230°C). Remove the
pots, reduce the heat to gas mark
2½–4, 320–350°F (160–180°C)
and bake for 10–15 minutes more.

LEAVEN

Mix a small quantity of barley
flour with warm water into a
dough. Form into a round shape
and make a dent in the centre to
go about half-way through. Put
the dough on a plate, cross it
lightly with a knife twice, and fill
the dent with warm water. Set it
aside for a few days when the
dough will have fermented and
split like an overripe fruit. It is
then ready to use as yeast to
'plum' the bread.

YORKSHIRE RIDDLE BREAD

Mix a quantity of pinhead
oatmeal with water to make a
thick porridge. Leave overnight
in a warm room. Next day add
salt to taste and place spoonfuls
on to a hot bakestone or griddle.
As the bread cooks it bubbles up,
giving a characteristic appearance.
Brown the cakes on one side only.

BIBLIOGRAPHY

Bulleid, A., *The Lake Villages of Somerset,* Glastonbury Antiquarian Society (Yeovil, 1924).

Clark, J.G.D., *Prehistoric England,* Batsford (London, 1940).

Clark, J.G.D., *Prehistoric Europe: the economic basis,* Methuen (London, 1952).

Danahar, K., *In Ireland Long Ago,* Mercier Press (Cork, 1962).

Evans, E.E., *Irish Folk Ways,* Routledge and Kegan Paul (London and Boston, 1957).

Firth, J., *Reminiscences of an Orkney Parish,* Rendall (Stromness, 1975).

Martin, M., *A description of the Western Isles of Scotland,* 1716, reprinted by Mercat Press (Edinburgh, 1976).

Megaw, J.V.S., and Simpson, D.D.A., *Introduction to British Prehistory,* Leicester University Press (Leicester, 1979).

Piggott, S., *The Neolithic Cultures of the British Isles,* Cambridge University Press (Cambridge, 1954).

Piggott, S., and Daniel, G., *Ancient British Art,* Cambridge University Press (Cambridge, 1951).

Tonnochy, A.B., *Later British Antiquities of the British Isles,* British Museum (London, 1953).

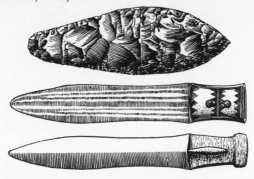

Flint knife and two bronze age knives

Food and Recipe Books

Ayrton, E., *The Cookery of England,* André Deutsch (London, 1974); Penguin Books (Harmondsworth, 1977).

Beeton, Mrs Isabella, *Mrs Beeton's Cookery and Household Management,* 1960 edition by Ward Lock, 82 Gower St, London WC1E 6EQ.

Cobbett, W., *Cottage Economy,* 1822, reprinted by Oxford University Press (Oxford, 1979).

David, E., *English Bread and Yeast Cookery,* Allen Lane and Penguin Books (Harmondsworth, 1977).

Drummond, J.C., and Wilbraham, A., *The Englishman's Food,* Jonathan Cape (London, 1939).

Grigson, G., *The Englishman's Flora,* Phoenix House (London, 1958); Paladin (St Albans, 1975).

Grigson, J., *English Food,* Macmillan (London, 1974); Penguin Books (Harmondsworth, 1977).

Grigson, J., *Jane Grigson's Fruit Book,* Michael Joseph (London, 1982); Penguin Books (Harmondsworth, 1983).

Hill, J., *The Wild Foods of Britain,* A. and C. Black (Publishers) Ltd (London, 1939).

Mabey, R., *Food for Free,* Collins (London, 1972); Fontana (London, 1976).

Phillips, R., *Wild Food,* Pan Books (London, 1983).

Richardson, R., *Hedgerow Cookery,* Penguin Books (Harmondsworth, 1980).

Simmons, J., *A Shetland Cook Book,* Thuleprint Ltd (Sandwick, Shetland, 1978).

Stout, M.B., *The Shetland Cookery Book,* T. and J. Manson (Lerwick, 1968).

Wilson, C.A., *Food and Drink in Britain,* Constable (London, 1973); Penguin Books (Harmondsworth, 1976).

RECIPE INDEX

Narrow-leaved Bittercress

Illustration acknowledgements:

A. Wetzel, ZEFA, *Prehistoric cave painting,* cover.
Botanical illustrations from British Flora, by Fitch and Smith,
L. Reeve & Co. London 1916.